Pre-reader

Helpers in Your Neighborhood

Shira Evans

NATIONAL GEOGRAPHIC

Washington, D.C.

Vocabulary Tree

MY NEIGHBORHOOD

PEOPLE

mail carrier
librarian
police officer
firefighter
waiter
teacher
doctor and nurse

PLACES

post office
library
police station
fire station
restaurant
school
hospital

We live in different places.

Many people work in our neighborhoods.

They help us every day.

Hi, I'm Hoshi.
I live in Japan.

In my neighborhood, the mail carrier brings letters.

He takes new letters
to the post office.

Hi, I'm Muni.
I live in India.

I go to the library
in my neighborhood.

The librarian helps
me find new books.

Hi, I'm Mateo.
I live in Chile.

In my neighborhood, police officers keep us safe.

At the police station, they talk
to people who need help.

In my neighborhood,
firefighters put out fires.

At the fire station, they get the
trucks ready for next time.

There is a restaurant in my neighborhood.

The waiter brings us food.
Pizza is my favorite!

At my school, the teacher knows a lot!

She helps us
read and write.

We go to the hospital
when we're sick.

Doctors and nurses
help us get better.

People work hard in our neighborhoods.

They help us stay
safe and happy.

YOUR TURN!

Draw your neighborhood. What helpers do you see when you go out?

park ranger

bus driver

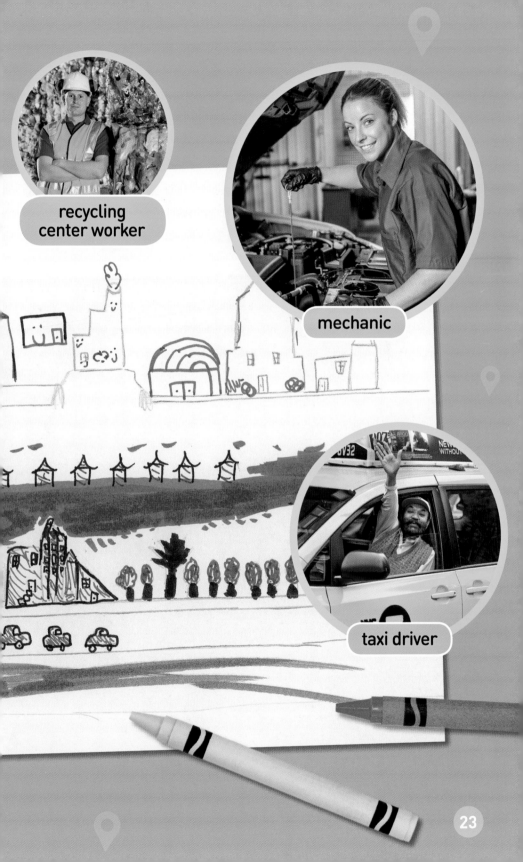

recycling center worker

mechanic

taxi driver

To Sam and Alex,
who continue to inspire me. —S.E.

AUTHOR'S NOTE: There are many kinds of helpers in the world! The helper on the cover of this book is a paramedic. She helps when people are hurt. The man on page 1 works on a community farm. He helps grow healthy food.

The author and publisher gratefully acknowledge the literacy review of this book by Kimberly Gillow, principal, Chelsea Schools, Michigan.

Published by National Geographic Partners, LLC, Washington, D.C. 20036. All rights reserved. Reproduction in whole or in part without written permission of the publisher is prohibited.

NATIONAL GEOGRAPHIC and Yellow Border Design are trademarks of the National Geographic Society, used under license.

Designed by Gus Tello

Library of Congress Cataloging-in-Publication Data
Names: Evans, Shira, author.
Title: Helpers in your neighborhood / by Shira Evans.
Description: Washington, DC : National Geographic Kids, 2018. | Series: National Geographic readers
Identifiers: LCCN 2018031442| ISBN 9781426332142 (pbk.) | ISBN 9781426332159 (hardcover)
Subjects: LCSH: Public safety--United States--Juvenile literature. | Neighborhoods--United States--Juvenile literature. | Communities--United States--Juvenile literature.
Classification: LCC HD4605 .E93 2018 | DDC 363.10023/73--dc23
LC record available at https://lccn.loc.gov/2018031442

Photo Credits

ASP = Alamy Stock Photo; GI = Getty Images

Cover, becon/GI; 1, Mint Images/Helen Norman/GI; 2 (LE), imtmphoto/GI; 2 (RT), Inti St Clair/GI; 3 (UP LE), Eric Lafforgue/ASP; 3 (UP RT), Visuals Stock/ASP; 3 (CTR LE), Nick Dolding/GI; 3 (CTR RT), imageBROKER/ASP; 3 (LO), Juanpablo San Martín/GI; 4, ollo/GI; 5, kali9/GI; 6 (LE), imtmphoto/GI; 6 (RT), NG Maps; 6-7, Matthias Tunger/GI; 8 (LE), Visuals Stock/ASP; 8 (RT), NG Maps; 8-9, Intellistudies/Shutterstock; 10 (LE), Juanpablo San Martín/GI; 10 (RT), NG Maps; 10-11, kemdim/Shutterstock; 12 (LE), Eric Lafforgue/ASP; 12 (RT), NG Maps; 12-13, Ken Gerhardt Photography/GI; 14 (LE), Inti St Clair/GI; 14 (RT), NG Maps; 14-15, andresr/GI; 16 (LE), imageBROKER/ASP; 16 (RT), NG Maps; 16-17, Stephanie Maze/GI; 18 (LE), Nick Dolding/GI; 18 (RT), NG Maps; 18-19, sturti/GI; 20, kali9/GI; 21, Adam Crowley/GI; 22 (UP), John Lund/Sam Diephuis/GI; 22 (LO), kali9/GI; 22-23 (crayons), Charles Brutlag/Dreamstime; 22-23 (drawing), Kaya Affan Dengel; 23 (UP LE), Echo/GI; 23 (UP RT), Lopolo/Shutterstock; 23 (CTR), maodesign/GI; 24, andresr/GI

National Geographic supports K–12 educators with ELA Common Core Resources. Visit natgeoed.org/commoncore for more information.

Printed in U.S.A.
18/WOR/1